MY FIRST BOOK OF
MICROBES

VIRUSES, BACTERIA, FUNGI, AND MORE

SHEDDAD KAID-SALAH FERRÓN
& EDUARD ALTARRIBA

Button
BOOKS

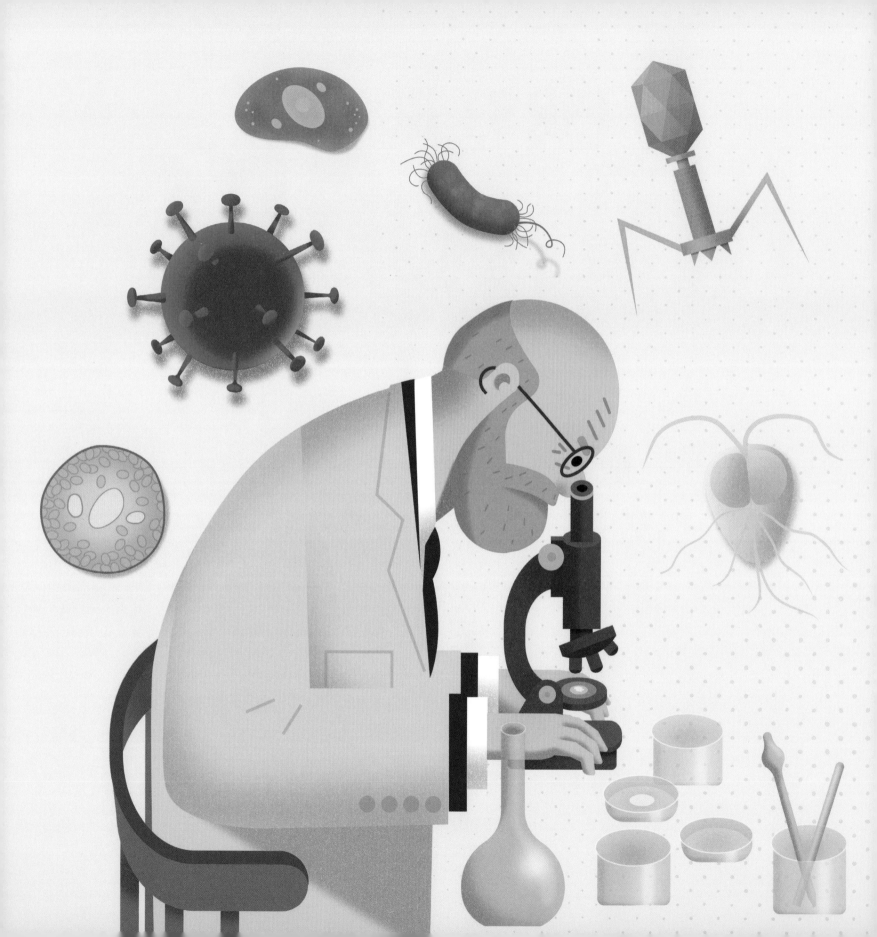

CONTENTS

INTRODUCTION

The word *microbe* comes from the Greek *mikrós*, meaning "*small*," and *bíos*, meaning "*life*."

Microbes or, as we also call them, microorganisms, are the smallest beings on Earth. They are so small that we cannot see them with the naked eye and we can only observe them under a microscope.

Microbes were the first inhabitants on Earth. The earliest microorganism fossils date back over 3.7 billion years ago and they are the oldest form of life we know.

We can find microbes everywhere: in our bodies, in plants, in food, and even in the most inhospitable places, such as fumaroles on the ocean bed, surviving at temperatures higher than 212°F (100°C), under the cold Antarctic ice, at less than 14°F (10°C below zero), or several miles/kilometers below the earth's surface with no light or oxygen.

Microbes are very important for life on our planet and without them we could not eat or breathe. Plants would have no nutrients to feed on either, and the oxygen in the atmosphere that we breathe would not exist. We also use them to produce food, such as cheese, bread, and yogurt, and to make medicines.

But not all microbes are good for us and some cause diseases in animals and plants.

Probably, in millions of years' time, as the Sun gets older and even hotter, microorganisms will be the last life forms to vanish from Earth when our planet starts to become uninhabitable.

WELCOME TO THE DIMINUTIVE WORLD OF THESE FASCINATING CREATURES!

BUT HOW BIG ARE MICROBES?

As we have said, organisms we cannot see with the naked eye are called microbes. They are very small and come in lots of different shapes and sizes.

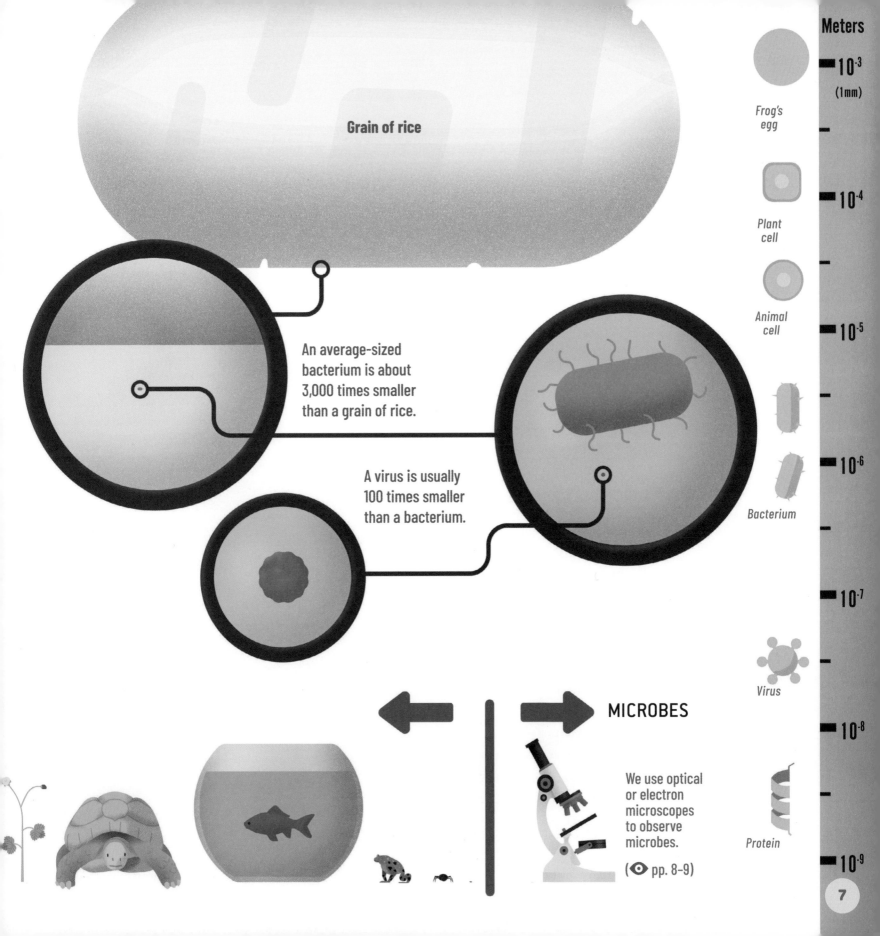

Grain of rice

An average-sized bacterium is about 3,000 times smaller than a grain of rice.

A virus is usually 100 times smaller than a bacterium.

MICROBES

We use optical or electron microscopes to observe microbes.

(👁 pp. 8–9)

Meters

10^{-3}
(1mm)

Frog's egg

10^{-4}

Plant cell

10^{-5}

Animal cell

10^{-6}

Bacterium

10^{-7}

10^{-8}

Virus

10^{-9}

Protein

MICROSCOPES

A microscope is an instrument we use to look at things too small to see with the naked eye. There are different types of microscopes, but they all do the same thing: they make an object bigger so we can look at it. Optical microscopes, the most common ones, use lenses to bend light and enlarge the image of the thing we want to see.

PEOPLE FIRST STARTED USING MICROSCOPES IN THE 16TH CENTURY. THANKS TO MICROSCOPES, ROBERT HOOKE DESCRIBED CELLS FOR THE FIRST TIME IN 1655.

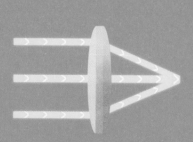

SIMPLE MICROSCOPE
16TH CENTURY

LENSES

A lens is a transparent optical mechanism that can bend light. Most lenses are made of glass. There are lots of kinds of lenses and they are used to make optical devices: glasses, telescopes, magnifying glasses, binoculars, etc. The lenses most often used in microscopes are those that focus light.

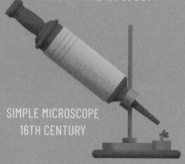

×10   ×100   ×500

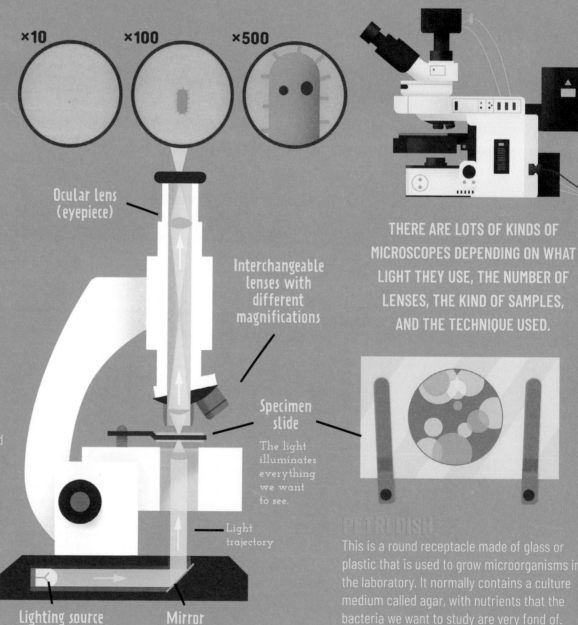

Ocular lens
(eyepiece)

Interchangeable lenses with different magnifications

THERE ARE LOTS OF KINDS OF MICROSCOPES DEPENDING ON WHAT LIGHT THEY USE, THE NUMBER OF LENSES, THE KIND OF SAMPLES, AND THE TECHNIQUE USED.

Specimen slide

The light illuminates everything we want to see.

Light trajectory

Lighting source   Mirror

PETRI DISH

This is a round receptacle made of glass or plastic that is used to grow microorganisms in the laboratory. It normally contains a culture medium called agar, with nutrients that the bacteria we want to study are very fond of.

Electron microscope

We can see much smaller things with an electron microscope than with an optical microscope; things such as viruses (👁 p. 30), for example.

Unlike an optical microscope that uses light, an electron microscope uses electrons to produce magnified images of tiny objects. It is a much more sophisticated and complex instrument than an optical microscope but it essentially does the same thing: it uses lenses to bend an electron beam and amplify the image of the thing we want to see.

As electrons cannot pass through glass, they use electromagnetic lenses—doughnut-shaped magnets that can bend electrons in the same way as a glass lens bends light.

Electrons are elementary particles found in the atoms that form matter.

(See *My First Book of Quantum Physics*, Sheddad Kaid-Salah Ferrón and Eduard Altarriba.)

This "cannon" fires electrons

CATHODE

ANODE

Electromagnetic lenses

Primary electron beam

Tower

Electromagnetic lenses

Specimen chamber

Detector

Secondary electrons

Specimen under observation

Vacuum chamber

Images of pollen grains captured by an electron microscope.

We can only see light with the naked eye, we can't see electrons. In modern electron microscopes we process the images of objects using a computer so we can see them magnified on a screen.

Computer for processing the image

Screen for visualizing the image

Storage systems

CELLS

All living beings are formed of cells, the basic units of life.

All cells are formed of a <u>casing</u> called a <u>cell membrane</u> that separates the cell from the outside; the <u>cytoplasm</u>, an aqueous internal substance that contains the other parts of the cell; and <u>genetic material</u>, the <u>DNA</u>, a large molecule that contains all the hereditary information and tells the cell what to do and how to behave.

There are two main types of cells.

Eukaryotic cells have a nucleus that contains the cell's genetic material (DNA). Prokaryotic cells, which are much simpler, don't have a nucleus and have genetic material floating around inside them.

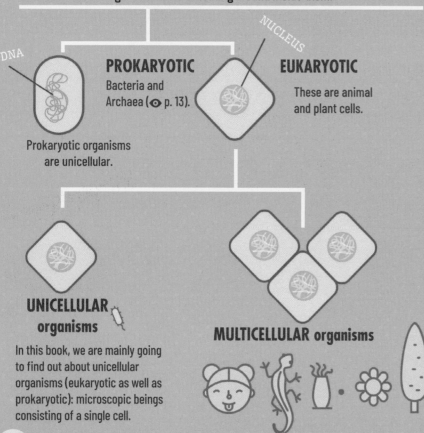

DNA

NUCLEUS

PROKARYOTIC
Bacteria and Archaea (👁 p. 13).

EUKARYOTIC
These are animal and plant cells.

Prokaryotic organisms are unicellular.

UNICELLULAR organisms

In this book, we are mainly going to find out about unicellular organisms (eukaryotic as well as prokaryotic): microscopic beings consisting of a single cell.

MULTICELLULAR organisms

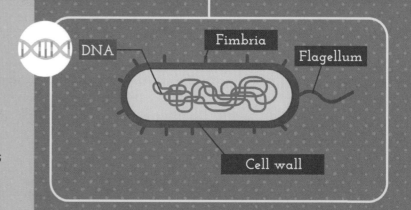

PROKARYOTIC CELL

DNA

Fimbria

Flagellum

Cell wall

EUKARYOTIC CELL

A eukaryotic cell is formed of:

1. The nucleus: contains the genetic material (DNA).

2. The plasma membrane: determines the boundaries of the cell and regulates the exchange of substances with the outside.

3. The cytoplasm: viscous liquid where the cell's components are found.

4. The organelles: located in the cytoplasm. Unlike prokaryotic cells, eukaryotic cells have specialized organelles that enable them to carry out various functions.

5. The cytoskeleton: the group of protein fibers that give the cell its shape.

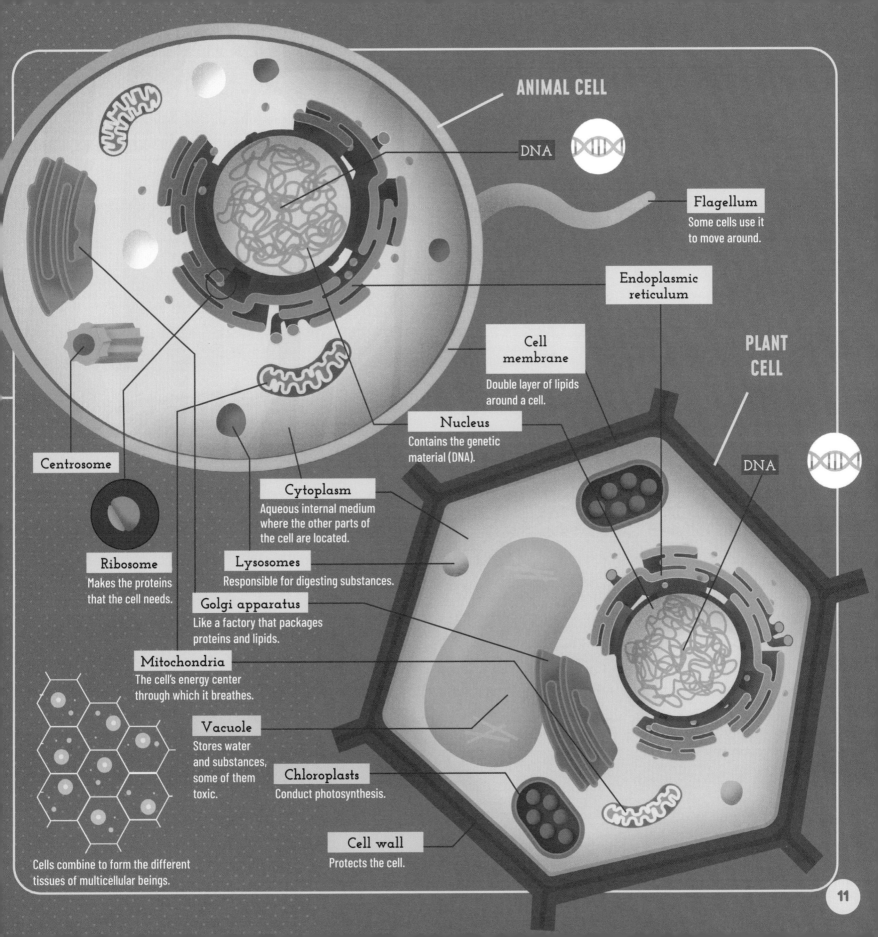

ANIMAL CELL

DNA

Flagellum
Some cells use it to move around.

Endoplasmic reticulum

PLANT CELL

DNA

Cell membrane
Double layer of lipids around a cell.

Nucleus
Contains the genetic material (DNA).

Centrosome

Ribosome
Makes the proteins that the cell needs.

Cytoplasm
Aqueous internal medium where the other parts of the cell are located.

Lysosomes
Responsible for digesting substances.

Golgi apparatus
Like a factory that packages proteins and lipids.

Mitochondria
The cell's energy center through which it breathes.

Vacuole
Stores water and substances, some of them toxic.

Chloroplasts
Conduct photosynthesis.

Cell wall
Protects the cell.

Cells combine to form the different tissues of multicellular beings.

11

TYPES OF MICROBES

Microbes are the smallest life form on Earth. There are many types of microbes, all very different from one another. The majority are UNICELLULAR individual organisms, formed of a single cell.

CELLULAR MICRO-ORGANISMS

PROKARYOTIC MICROORGANISMS

These are microbes that consist of a very simple **single cell** called **prokaryotic**. Prokaryotic cells **are the most primitive cells**. Their main characteristic is that they do not have a nucleus and the genetic material (DNA) is free in the cell's cytoplasm.

DNA

EUKARYOTIC MICROORGANISMS

These are microbes **formed by eukaryotic cells** containing genetic material (DNA) inside a membranous envelope **that forms the cell's nucleus**. Eukaryotic cells are also the cells in **animals and plants**.

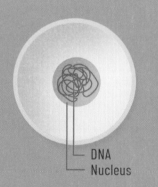

DNA
Nucleus

ACELLULAR MICRO-ORGANISMS

VIRUSES

Viruses are a special type of microorganism as **they are not even a cell** (they are acellular). Many scientists do not consider them to be a life form as they do not grow or feed. Besides this, **they need to infect the cell of another organism in order to multiply.** They are the smallest of all microbes.

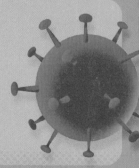

BACTERIA

They are **the most abundant life form** on our planet and we can find them almost everywhere. They can be different sizes and shapes: they can be round, elongated, spiral, etc. Many of them are good for us, but some can be **pathogenic and cause diseases**.

ARCHAEA

They are very similar to bacteria, although **they can "eat" things that bacteria cannot**. There are archaea capable of living in **extreme environments** where other organisms cannot survive. One key characteristic of archaea is that they are not pathogenic, so **they do not cause disease**.

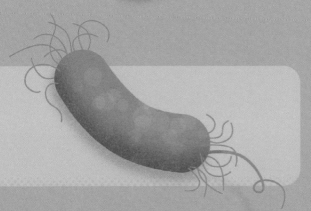

FUNGI

These include **yeasts** that we use to make bread, and the **mold** that rots (decomposes) fruit. Fungi have the ability to form **long filaments of more than one cell**.

ALGAE

Many algae are **unicellular** and, like plants, they can conduct **photosynthesis**; thanks to the **chlorophyll** contained in their cells, they can use the Sun's light to obtain energy.

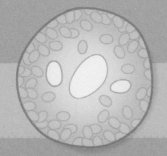

PROTOZOANS

They are a bit like **unicellular animals**, formed by a single cell. They usually live in damp environments and are capable of **moving and "feeding" on other organisms**.

BACTERIA

Bacteria are one of the most important groups of living organisms on Earth. They are the most abundant living beings and it has been calculated that across the entire planet there are approximately 1,000,000,000,000,000,000,000,000,000,000 (1 followed by 30 zeros). **Bacteria** are essential for humans and for the ecology of the planet.

There are so many bacteria on Earth that together they weigh more than all the plants and animals on the planet.

Are they bad for us?

Although there are pathogenic bacteria that can cause diseases, the majority of bacteria do not pose any danger to us. In fact, it has been calculated that we all have approximately 2lb (1kg) of microbes in or on our body, and don't think this is a bad thing: without them we could not survive ( p. 21).

Where are the bacteria?

Everywhere. They are on the ground, in the sky, in the water, underground, and even in your skin, your hair, and inside you.

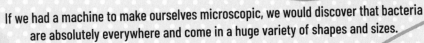
If we had a machine to make ourselves microscopic, we would discover that bacteria are absolutely everywhere and come in a huge variety of shapes and sizes.

Anatomy of a bacterium

A bacterium is a living organism formed by a single PROKARYOTIC CELL.
Prokaryotic cells are the simplest cells that exist and their main characteristic, in contrast to eukaryotic cells, is that the genetic material containing hereditary information, or DNA, is dispersed around the cell's cytoplasm instead of being stored inside a nucleus. (👁 pp. 10–11).

The CELL WALL is a rigid and resistant layer of protection found around the cell membrane. It gives the cell its shape.

The NUCLEOID is the region that contains the genetic information, the coiled DNA molecule, which is in the cytoplasm.

The RIBOSOMES are the cell's protein factories. When a cell needs to "manufacture" a protein, it sends the information from the DNA to a ribosome via a messenger. There, the amino acids, the protein building blocks, group together and assemble themselves following the instructions they have been given.

The FLAGELLUM is a mobile appendage shaped like a whip, present in some bacteria, which the cell uses to move around.

The CELL or PLASMA MEMBRANE is a layer consisting of two sheets (bilayer). It allows nutrients from the outside environment to enter the cell and waste substances to leave.

The CYTOPLASM is the liquid substance inside the cell membrane where the organelles and the nucleoid are found.

PILI are also hairy appendages, longer than fimbriae and shorter than flagella. Bacteria mostly use them for passing genetic information among themselves.

FIMBRIAE are like hairs on the outside of many bacteria and they are used to adhere to different surfaces.

A PLASMID is a circular molecule of DNA that acts independently.

TYPES OF BACTERIA

Bacteria are hugely diverse. There are thousands of species of bacteria with their own characteristics and peculiarities.

Some are benign, while others cause diseases (pathogenic), some need oxygen to live (aerobic), and others don't (anaerobic), some have no flagellum, and others have one or several flagella.

With so many different types of bacteria, it is not easy to classify them. One way to do it is by their shape and how they group together.

There are three main shapes:

BACILLI

These are elongated bacteria, shaped like a rod (*Lactobacillus*).

We can also find bacillus in groups:

Diplobacilli
A pair of bacilli
(*Klebsiella pneumoniae*)

Streptobacilli
Chains of bacilli
(*Streptobacillus moniliformis*)

SPIRAL BACTERIA

These are spiral or helical bacteria.

(*Treponema pallidum*)

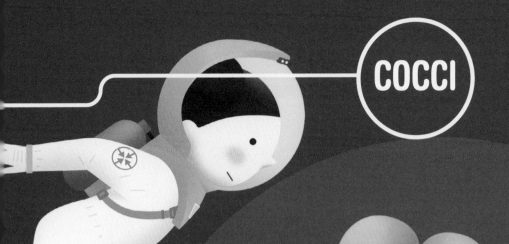

COCCI

These are spherical-shaped bacteria, like a ball.

Cocci can exist as individual cells, although they can also group together as:

Diplococci
In pairs
(*Neisseria gonorrhoeae*)

Staphylococci
Groups of cocci in a cluster shape—bacteria divide in any direction
(*Staphylococcus epidermidis*)

Tetracocci
Four by four
(*Micrococcus antarcticus*)

Streptococci
Chains of cocci—bacteria divide along a single axis
(*Streptococcus agalactiae*)

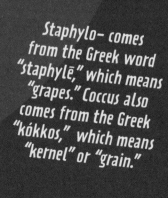

Staphylo- comes from the Greek word "staphylē," which means "grapes." Coccus also comes from the Greek "kókkos," which means "kernel" or "grain."

BACTERIAL REPRODUCTION

Bacteria are very simple organisms. Basically, they spend their time feeding, growing, and multiplying.

HOW THEY REPRODUCE

Bacteria replicate or reproduce through binary fission or bipartition; each bacteria divides into two cells generating two identical bacteria.

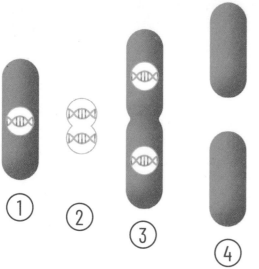

① Bacteria grow as they feed and absorb nutrients from their surroundings.

② When a bacterium reaches a certain size, it makes a copy of its DNA, its genetic material.

③ Each molecule of the DNA goes to opposite sides, and the mother cell divides into two daughter cells, sharing out the material it contained.

④ From a single bacterium, two identical daughter bacteria are formed.*

*Well, they are not always identical. Sometimes, bacteria make little mistakes when they copy the DNA and the genetic information varies a bit. When this happens, some of the new bacteria are slightly different from the original ones. We say that they have mutated (👁 p. 46).

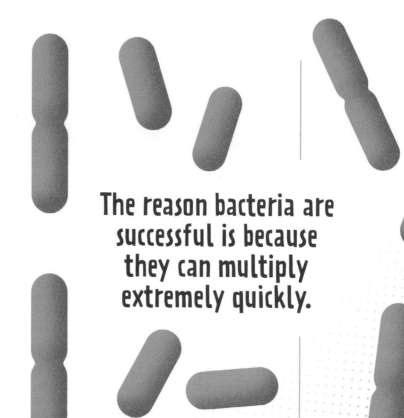

The reason bacteria are successful is because they can multiply extremely quickly.

To give you an idea, the *Escherichia coli* bacteria reproduces itself every 20 minutes.

In other words, in 20 minutes a single bacterium becomes 2 bacteria; in 40 minutes it becomes 4; after 60 minutes (1 hour), it becomes 8. Every hour there would be 8 times more bacteria.

It doesn't seem like much, does it? Let's take a look at what happens...

1 h
8 bacteria

2 h
64 bacteria

3 h
512 bacteria

4 h
4,096 bacteria

5 h
32,768 bacteria

They grow

The food
runs out

Lots
of food

They die

Bacteria are not immortal, nor do they grow indefinitely. As soon as conditions are unfavorable and the food runs out, they stop growing and start to die.

WE ARE NOT ALONE

Although you can't see them, we are always accompanied by billions of invisible beings that live on and in us. They've been doing this for millions of years and without these secret lodgers, we would not survive.

Part of our microbiota is found in the skin, mouth, nasal passages, ears, eyes, lungs, vagina, and digestive tract.

90% of our microbiota is found in the intestines (this is usually called gut flora).

ALL MICROBES THAT LIVE IN OR ON ANOTHER ORGANISM ARE CALLED MICROBIOTA OR MICROBIOME.

The vast majority of our lodgers are benign and we exist in symbiosis with them. In other words, we need them and they need us to survive, although on occasion they can pose a danger.

For example, bacteria in our mouth can cause tooth decay if we do not brush our teeth regularly.

2lb

Between 7oz (200g) and 2lb (1kg) of our body weight is made up of the bacteria we are carrying.

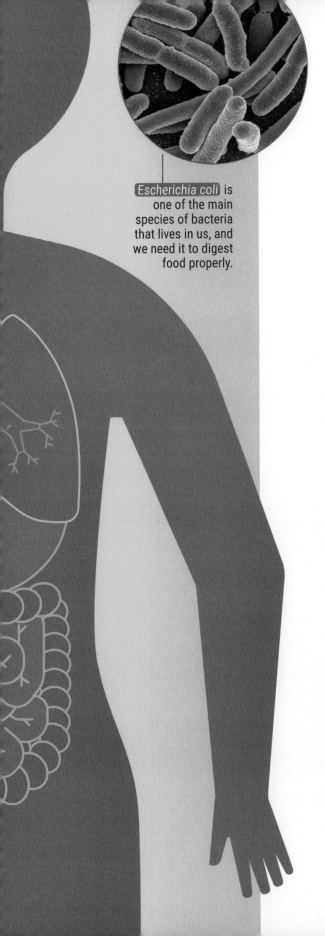

Escherichia coli is one of the main species of bacteria that lives in us, and we need it to digest food properly.

LOOK AFTER YOUR MICROBES

WE ARE A WALKING ECOSYSTEM, HOME TO BILLIONS OF MICROORGANISMS OF OVER 10,000 SPECIES WITH WHICH WE CO-EXIST.

A VERY PERSONAL MICROBIOTA

We don't all have the same microbes and we all have our own microbiota that changes throughout our lives. When we are born, we acquire part of our mother's microbiota and as we grow up, our microbiota evolves, especially due to our diet, our personal hygiene, and that of the people or animals around us.

Every day we exchange all kinds of microbes with our family, our friends, and even our pets.

TEAMWORK

Microbes are essential for our health and they accompany us throughout our life. Our microbiota makes it difficult for pathogenic bacteria to colonize us, helps us to digest food, manufactures vitamins, and influences the nutrients our body absorbs.

We need a varied and balanced diet for a healthy microbiota.

The human microbiota is all the microorganisms that live in or on our body. The majority are bacteria, although we can also find archaea, fungi, and viruses.

ARCHAEA

Archaea are unicellular microorganisms very similar to bacteria. They are so similar that, when they were first discovered not that long ago, in 1977, it was thought they were a special type of bacteria.

Archaea might be the first life forms to have lived on Earth. Their name, archaea, comes from the Greek "*arkhaía*," meaning "ancient" or "primitive."

Cell wall

Fimbria

Plasmid

Nucleoid (DNA)

Cell membrane

Ribosome

Flagellum

Archaea are prokaryotic and, like bacteria, their cells have no nucleus or organelles. But, despite their initial appearance, we now know **they are very different from bacteria.**

For example, archaea's cell membranes are very different from those of all other cells; archaea have **a very resistant membrane** that, in some cases, seems to give them superpowers.

The way they obtain energy and feed themselves is very varied. **They are capable of feeding on almost anything** and they can even obtain energy from sunlight.

Physics and chemistry

Archaea carry out a huge number of processes related to several different chemical elements, such as sulphur, carbon, or nitrogen. Scientists are studying how to use them for manufacturing and medical purposes.

Different shapes

They come in many different shapes, some of which are like bacteria: circular (cocci), cylindrical (bacilli), spiral, and irregular. *Haloquadratum walsbyi* is a square-shaped archaea.

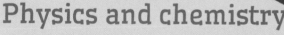

LIVING ON THE EDGE

Archaea started populating the Earth when the oxygen-rich atmosphere that we breathe did not yet exist. Thanks to their resistant membrane and their ability to adapt for feeding and obtaining energy in very varied ways, archaea can live almost anywhere. In fact, many live in EXTREME environments, where no other "creature" is able to survive. We can find them in areas with no oxygen, in extremely salty environments, in extremely acidic waters, or at very high temperatures. They are said to be EXTREMOPHILE organisms (although they are not the only ones, as some bacteria are also extremophile).

Hydrothermal vents are one of the most extreme environments on our planet. They are usually found in the depths of the ocean, where sunlight does not reach.

These underwater fumaroles are found in areas where there are active volcanoes and they expel minerals and water heated by the magma of the Earth's mantle. The temperature of the water emerging from them can be up to 752°F (400°C).

In this dark environment of extreme pressure and high temperatures, we can find archaea that feed on the minerals expelled by the hydrothermal vents.

ARCHAEA DO NOT CAUSE DISEASES.

Where can we find them?

Very cold environments

Acidic waters

On the ground

In living beings

FUNGI

Fungi are eukaryotic organisms whose main characteristic is that their cells have a cellular wall formed partly by a substance called chitin.* Fungi have no cilia (small hairs) or flagella, and cannot move around by themselves.

*Algae and plants also have a cell wall but theirs is made of cellulose.

LIVING FROM THE LAND

Unlike plants and algae (👁 p. 28), which manufacture their own food through photosynthesis (they are **autotrophs**), fungi are NOT capable of producing their food and have to look for it in the environment around them, which makes them **heterotrophs** like animals and protozoa.

Fungi **are hugely** diverse, from unicellular yeasts to multicellular fungi, such as molds and mushrooms. They can be very beneficial or harmful. They are essential for life on the planet. Scientists who study fungi are mycologists.

Chitin also forms part of the exoskeletons of insects, spiders, and the hard shells of crabs.

Bud scar

Cell wall

Vacuole

Mitochondria

Plasma membrane

Nucleus

Fungi are very important for ecosystems because, along with bacteria, they are the main organisms that decompose dead organic material.

Molds **are a type of** multicellular fungus **and they are what makes fruit rot and bread go moldy. They are formed by long threads of cells called** hyphae. **If you look very closely at moldy bread, you can see something like fluff; this is a clump of branching and intertwined mold hyphae that forms a tangle of filaments we call** mycelium.

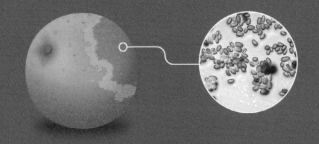

YEAST

Yeasts **are a type of** unicellular **fungus used in food to carry out** fermentation*: **they can convert sugars into other substances, such as alcohol or carbon (CO_2).**

For example, *Saccharomyces cerevisiae* is a yeast that ferments sugar into alcohol and is used to make beer and wine.

Yeasts are also used to make bread. They are added to the bread dough and left to rest. The yeasts then convert (ferment) sugars into CO_2: the gas that creates bubbles inside the dough and makes it light and airy when it is baked in the oven.

Louis Pasteur (👁 p. 41) showed that microorganisms such as yeast or bacteria cause fermentation.

Some fungi can also be pathogenic. Infections caused by fungi are called mycoses.
An example of mycosis is "athlete's foot," a skin infection on the toes caused by a fungus called *dermatophytes*. These fungi love damp patches of skin where there is no airflow. They really like sweaty non-breathable shoes.

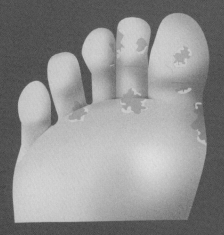

Fungi can also be used to make medicines; in fact, penicillin, the first antibiotic to be discovered, was made from the fungus
Penicillium notatum
(👁 p. 45).

Fungi are essentially land-based. Many are pathogenic, and they infect animals and plants, although some also establish beneficial relationships with other organisms.

PROTOZOA

They are small organisms with a single eukaryotic cell (unicellular).

CYTOPLASM

GOLGI APPARATUS

ENDOPLASMIC RETICULUM

DNA

NUCLEUS

Their cells have a nucleus and organelles with a membrane, and they are similar to plant and animal cells.

MICRONUCLEUS

RIBOSOME

MITOCHONDRIA

VACUOLE

CILIUM

AQUATIC BEINGS

Protozoa live freely in aquatic environments (saltwater or freshwater) or as parasites inside other living beings.

CONTRACTILE VACUOLE

CELL MEMBRANE

OCEANS

RIVERS AND LAKES

INSIDE OTHER BEINGS

The majority of protozoa feed by "hunting" other living beings, such as bacteria, algae, yeasts, or other smaller protozoa.

AMOEBAE

An amoeba lives freely in water and feeds on smaller organisms. It is like a kind of jelly that constantly changes shape thanks to its "amoeboid" movement: it uses pseudopods (projections of the cytoplasm) to move.

LYSOSOME   BACTERIUM   DIGESTIVE VACUOLE   REMAINS

PSEUDOPOD

When it detects its victim, it uses the pseudopods to engulf its prey and phagocytize (ingest or devour) it.

Once inside, the food is digested thanks to substances called "enzymes" in its lysosomes.

GIARDIA

This protozoan with flagella is a parasite that lives in the human intestine and causes a disease called giardiasis.

It feeds by sticking to the cells of the intestine and eating food passing through.

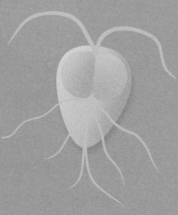

PARAMECIUM

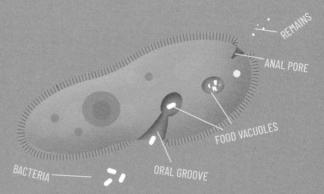

REMAINS

ANAL PORE

FOOD VACUOLES

BACTERIA   ORAL GROOVE

A paramecium has lots of small hairs called cilia on its surface. Each hair generates a slight movement, enabling the paramecium to move around.

It is quite big for a microorganism and lives freely in stagnant freshwater. It has an oral cavity for a mouth through which it "swallows" its victims, mainly microorganisms smaller than itself. Once it has digested them, it expels the waste outside the cell.

PLASMODIUM

Plasmodium is an "immobile" protozoan that lives as a parasite in blood and is transmitted through Anopheles mosquitoes. It causes malaria, a disease affecting millions of people around the world.

ALGAE

Algae are eukaryotic aquatic beings that, like plants, can conduct PHOTOSYNTHESIS, the natural process that enables them to extract energy from the Sun to make their own food: they are AUTOTROPHIC organisms.

Despite their huge diversity, they can be classified according to their color as green algae, red algae, and brown algae.

Some are gigantic, they can be up to 164ft (50m) in length and form underwater forests; others are unicellular organisms, consisting of a single eukaryotic cell.

OCEANS **FRESHWATER**

LIVING FROM THE SUN

PHOTOSYNTHESIS is the process algae and plants use to convert sunlight into the energy they need to live.

To do this, they use CHLOROPHYLL, a green-colored pigment found in cell organelles called chloroplasts.

The Sun's energy is captured in the chloroplasts, and carbon from the atmosphere (CO_2) and water (H_2O) are used to make glucose, the food that algae and plants use as fuel, enabling them to carry out their vital functions—growing, reproducing, etc.

This process also releases the oxygen (O_2) that we breathe into the atmosphere.

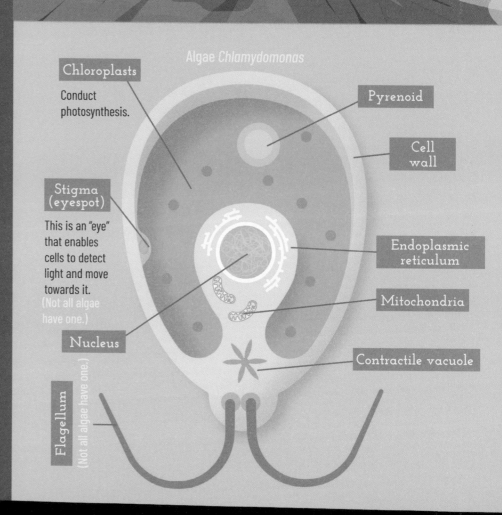

Algae *Chlamydomonas*

Chloroplasts
Conduct photosynthesis.

Pyrenoid

Cell wall

Stigma (eyespot)
This is an "eye" that enables cells to detect light and move towards it. (Not all algae have one.)

Endoplasmic reticulum

Mitochondria

Nucleus

Contractile vacuole

Flagellum (Not all algae have one.)

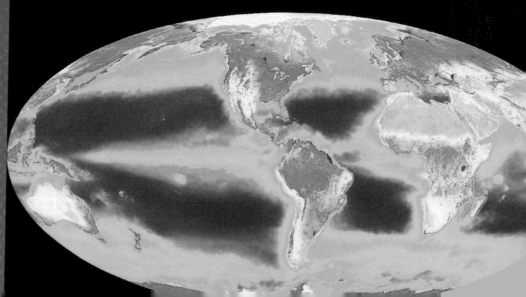

PHYTOPLANKTON

UNICELLULAR ALGAE form part of PHYTOPLANKTON, the group of autotrophic aquatic organisms that float in freshwater or saltwater. Phytoplankton are very important for life on Earth because they are food for many aquatic animals and are also responsible for around 50% of the oxygen in the atmosphere.

Diatoms are the most common group of unicellular algae in phytoplankton. There are around 20,000 species and some have spectacular shapes and geometrical patterns.

CYANOBACTERIA

Cyanobacteria are also types of phytoplankton. They look very like unicellular algae: they are autotrophic microbes, capable of carrying out photosynthesis but, unlike the latter, they are prokaryotic cells, which is what makes them bacteria.

Cyanobacteria are very old; they originated around 3.7 billion years ago. They populated the early oceans, where only microscopic life existed. They were the first photosynthetic beings and it was thanks to them that the oxygen we animals breathe was released into the atmosphere.

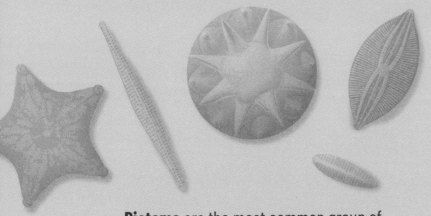

Image showing the planetary distribution of photosynthesis conducted by phytoplankton in the oceans and also by land plants.

The cell wall of diatoms is hard and porous, and it forms a very firm, glassy shell called a frustule.

MAXIMUM CHLOROPHYLL CONCENTRATION:

- at sea
- on land

For over 2 billion years, photosynthesis happened in the oceans, until the emergence of land plants descended from green algae.

VIRUSES

We've all heard of viruses. They are responsible for many infections and diseases, from a common cold to flu and even much more serious things. But what actually are viruses?

They are SMALL

Viruses are some of the tiniest microbes in existence, **and on average are around 100 times smaller than bacteria.**

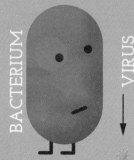

BACTERIUM

VIRUS

They are ACELLULAR

Viruses are not even cells; they do not contain cellular structures like bacteria or eukaryotic cells. That means they don't have mitochondria or a nucleus, or ribosomes, or membranes, or chloroplasts, etc.

They are just DNA or RNA molecules surrounded by a layer of proteins.

Double-stranded DNA

Single-stranded RNA

GENETIC MATERIAL

Can be DNA or RNA.

CAPSID

Protein shell that protects the genetic material.

VIRAL ENVELOPE

Some have this envelope that protects them from the outside (when they are not inside a cell). It is a lipid layer that comes from the cytoplasm membrane of the host cell.

The word VIRUS comes from the Latin "virus," meaning "toxic" or "poison."

Viruses are NOT living beings

As viruses are not cellular organisms, most scientists do not consider viruses to be LIFE as they do not perform the basic functions that a living being must do autonomously:

They don't reproduce by themselves.

They don't feed by themselves.

They don't interact among themselves.

So, HOW DO THEY DO ALL THAT?

THEY ARE PARASITES

In order to reproduce, **viruses** infect a living cell **and use the cellular structures of the infected or host cell** to make copies of themselves.

Viruses can infect eukaryotic cells, **such as animal, plant, or fungi cells,** or prokaryotic cells, **such as bacteria or archaea cells.**

Viruses that infect bacteria **are called** bacteriophages **or, simply, phages. Phages can be used instead of antibiotics to treat bacterial infections** [ p. 34 and p. 44]. **If we want to eliminate pathogenic bacteria, we can use bacteriophage viruses to kill them.**

How a virus infects a cell

When a virus invades a cell it inserts its genetic material into it and it cancels the cell's genetic information. The cell is then hijacked and converted into a virus factory that can replicate many copies of the virus. The newly manufactured viruses leave the cell and infect other cells that, in turn, produce more viruses.

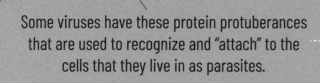

Some viruses have these protein protuberances that are used to recognize and "attach" to the cells that they live in as parasites.

Types of viruses

Viruses come in many different shapes and sizes. There are bigger ones and smaller ones. Their capsid can be cylindrical, helical, icosahedral (20 faces), or an even more complex shape. Some have an envelope while others don't (we refer to them as "naked").

What's more, viruses can also have genetic material in the form of a DNA molecule, like cells, although there are viruses that store their genetic material in a very particular way, in the form of an RNA molecule, which is different to other microbes.

Viruses can infect fungi, animals, and plants, as well as bacteria and archaea. Each virus tends to specialize in infecting one or various types of cells, causing different effects and diseases in the infected organisms.

Hepatovirus

Herpesvirus
> herpes

Adenovirus

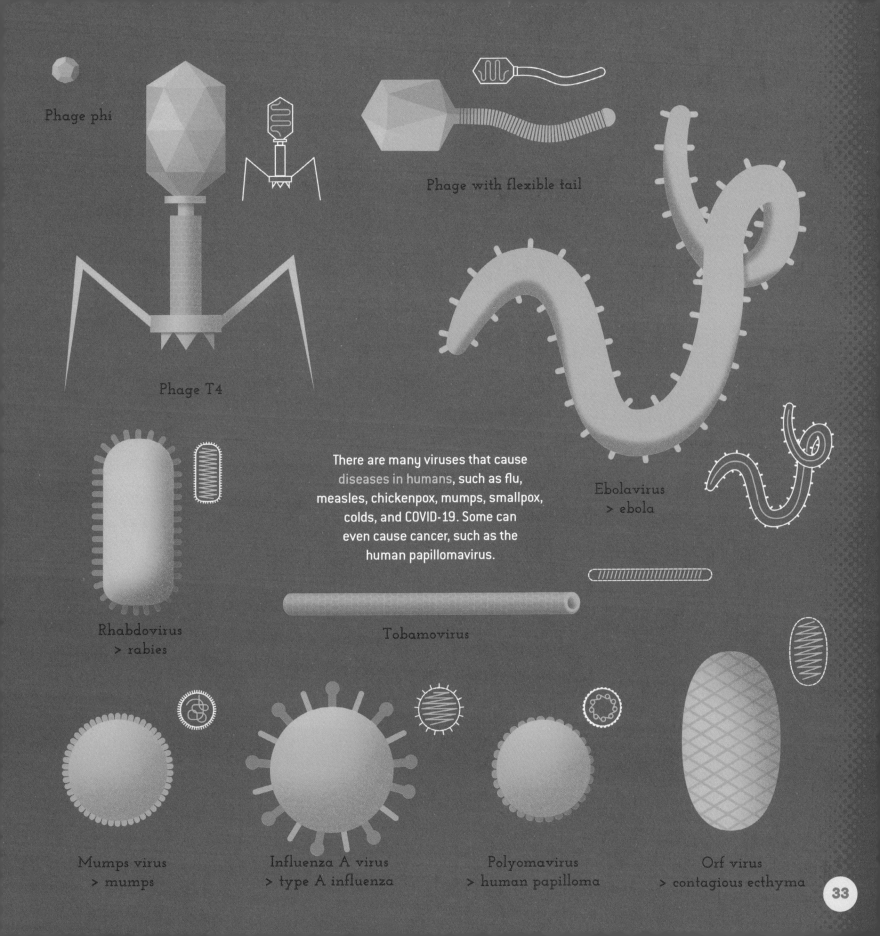

Phage phi

Phage T4

Phage with flexible tail

Ebolavirus
> ebola

There are many viruses that cause diseases in humans, such as flu, measles, chickenpox, mumps, smallpox, colds, and COVID-19. Some can even cause cancer, such as the human papillomavirus.

Rhabdovirus
> rabies

Tobamovirus

Mumps virus
> mumps

Influenza A virus
> type A influenza

Polyomavirus
> human papilloma

Orf virus
> contagious ecthyma

33

HOW DOES A VIRUS INFECT A CELL?

For a virus to infect a cell, it first has to "come alongside" to attach to it. It does this by latching on to the cell's surface through receptors in the cell's plasma membrane that enable the virus to anchor to the cell.

But not all receptors let the virus enter, only a few very specific ones. Each membrane receptor is like a single lock that allows entry into the cell. Each virus has a key that can only open one type of lock. If the key does not match, the virus cannot enter.

This means that not all viruses can infect any cell; they can only infect the ones they can enter.

Once the virus inserts its genetic material (DNA or RNA), it orders the cell to manufacture copies of the virus that can go on to infect other cells.

PHAGES

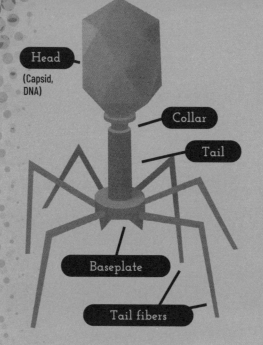

Head (Capsid, DNA)

Collar

Tail

Baseplate

Tail fibers

This amazing-looking virus is a bacteriophage, also called a phage, a type of virus that specializes in "hacking" bacteria to reproduce.

Every day, phages and bacteria wage a war that causes trillions of victims all around us without us realizing.

We can see how a T4 phage infects an *Escherichia Coli* (E. Coli) bacteria:

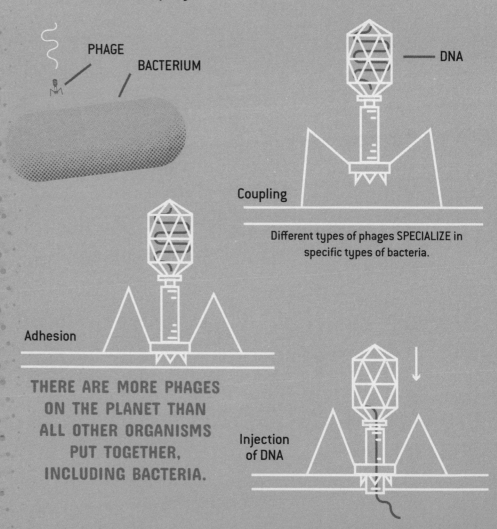

PHAGE

BACTERIUM

DNA

Coupling

Different types of phages SPECIALIZE in specific types of bacteria.

Adhesion

Injection of DNA

THERE ARE MORE PHAGES ON THE PLANET THAN ALL OTHER ORGANISMS PUT TOGETHER, INCLUDING BACTERIA.

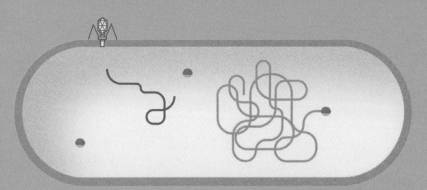

1 As we already know, a bacterium has its own DNA, the genetic code that tells the bacterium what it is—its shape, function, etc.—kind of like an instruction manual.

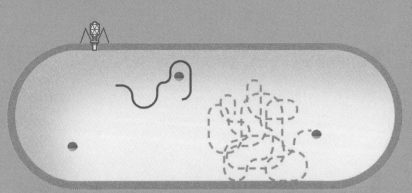

2 Once the cell has been infected, its DNA degrades and it starts synthesizing the phage's DNA. The virus has taken control of the cell *(3 mins)*.

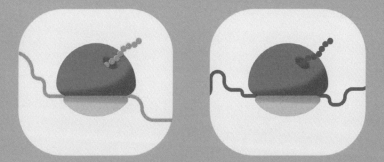

Ribosomes are small protein "factories." Their job is to read the lines of RNA code with the bacterium's genetic instructions for making proteins, which will become the "parts" that the cell needs.

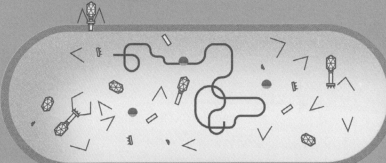

3 The cell's ribosomes work for the virus, manufacturing proteins to make more viruses *(9 mins)*. These proteins then create the *"parts"*—the heads and the tails—of the new viruses *(12 mins)*.

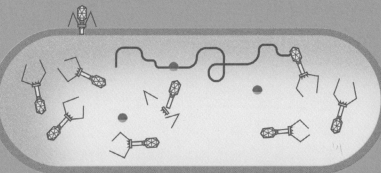

4 The heads are filled with the virus's DNA and all the parts are assembled. The new viruses are now ready *(15 mins)*.

And this whole process takes less than half an hour!

5 Finally, the viruses produce substances that make the cell explode (lyse), releasing hundreds of viruses ready to infect other bacteria *(22 mins)*.

MICROBIAL BIOTECHNOLOGY

Humans have always lived with microorganisms, and we have learned to get on well with many of them, such as the ones in our microbiota.

Not all microbes are pathogenic. We have used some to our advantage for thousands of years; for example, to make food or medicine. Now that we have improved the technology, and microbiologists know much more about microbes, we can use them in numerous areas to benefit us and the environment.

FOOD

As we have already seen (👁 p. 25), fermentation is the process that converts sugars into other substances such as alcohol, CO_2, or lactic acid. To carry out fermentation, we use different microorganisms, such as yeasts or bacteria.

Bread is one of the oldest foods made by humans. A bakery was known to exist in ancient Egypt in 2,575 BCE. To make bread, yeasts are added to the bread dough so that CO_2 gas is produced inside the dough, giving it a nice soft texture.

Cheese is another of the oldest foods. It was first produced around 8,000 years ago. There are thousands of types of cheese and they all come from the lactic fermentation of milk that produces curd. By separating the curd from the liquid and leaving it to rest, we get cheese. To ferment the milk, we use various bacteria, such as *Lactobacillus* and *Bifidobacterium*. If we add spore from the *Penicillum roqueforti* fungus, we get Roquefort cheese, with its characteristic smell, texture, and flavor.

To make **wine**, we press grapes to get the grape juice or must, and we leave it to rest. Along with yeasts, the microorganisms in the grape skins are what makes the must ferment so that we get the alcoholic drink.

AGRICULTURE

One of the biggest problems for agriculture is the plagues of insects that can ruin entire harvests. Microbes can be used as bioinsecticides to control plagues. Bacteria, viruses, and fungi are used to eliminate specific insects.

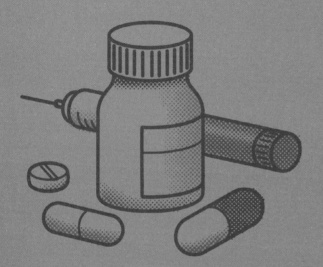

MEDICINE

Many microbial products contribute to animal and human well-being. One example of this is the medications we make with genetically modified bacteria and fungi. We can make antibiotics, hormones such as insulin (very important for diabetics), and anti-tumor drugs to treat cancer.

THE ENVIRONMENT

Oil spills in the ocean are an ecological disaster. To clean an oil spill, we use a kind of bacteria that feed on the hydrocarbons petrol is made of. We usually add other nutrients that these bacteria like. In this way, the bacteria "eat up" the spill faster and accelerate the decomposition of the petrol so it doesn't damage the ocean as much.

These are just some of the many examples of the benefits of using microorganisms. In any case, we have to be careful when we use microbes in biotechnology because if we use them incorrectly, they can lead to undesired effects over the long-term, such as the emergence of antibiotic-resistant pathogens.

"MINI" MULTICELLULAR ORGANISMS

Not all microscopic organisms are unicellular. There are loads of incredible beings that can only be seen under a microscope and are found everywhere, including in your skin and your hair.

EYELASH MITES These inoffensive beings live on people's faces and eyelashes, and are more common than you might think. They feed on the substances we secrete through the pores in our skin and through the glands around the eyes.

NEMATODES
Many species of nematodes are microscopic. These worms live everywhere, from oceans to inside your body as parasites.

DUST MITES
These microscopic animals are directly related to spiders and ticks. They feed on flakes of skin and multiply in the fibers of home textiles: sofas, carpets, mattresses, etc.

Dust mites do not bite or transmit disease, although they can cause allergies.

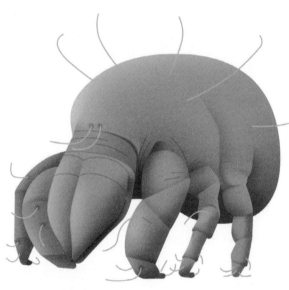

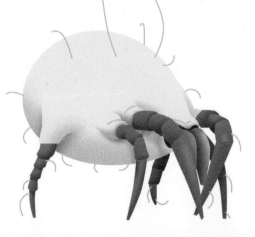

WATER BEARS OR "MOSS PIGLETS"

TARDIGRADES

Tardigrades, also known as "water bears" because of the way they move, can be found in almost all habitats on the planet, from the Arctic expanses to deserts, jungles, and gardens.

They are mostly land-based and usually live in the moisture on mosses, lichens, and ferns, although they can also live in freshwater and oceans (saltwater).

302°F (150°C)

-328°F (-200°C)

A tardigrade is about 1/64in (0.5mm) in size and consists of around 1,000 cells.

SUPERPOWERS

They are extremophile organisms; in other words, they have "superpowers" that enable them to live in extreme conditions. They can survive very high pressures, temperatures ranging from -328°F (-200°C) to 302°F (150°C), prolonged periods of dehydration (they can go for up to 10 years without water), toxic environments, areas with radiation, and even the vacuum in space.

The tiny water bears need a fine layer of water around their bodies to carry out the activities necessary to sustain life, but if the conditions change and they find themselves in a dry environment, tardigrades are able to enter a kind of dormant state called cryptobiosis: they retract their head and their eight legs, shrivel up into a kind of small ball and become dehydrated (expelling nearly all the water in their body), entering a death-like state of suspended animation.

They can remain in this state for decades, waiting to be submerged in water once again so they can come back to life.

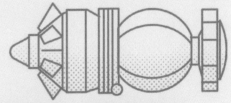

SPACE COWBOYS

In 2007, ESA* exposed some tardigrades for 12 days on the surface of the Russian spacecraft Foton-M3, and they survived the space journey.

In 2011, NASA** did the same, putting them on the outside of the space shuttle Endeavour, and the little bears once again survived the vacuum, cosmic rays, and ultraviolet radiation.

*ESA: European Space Agency
**NASA: National Aeronautics and Space Administration (USA)

INFECTIONS

Germs are pathogenic organisms: microbes capable of causing disease in other organisms.

An infection is when germs invade and multiply in our bodies. The germs that cause infections can be bacteria, viruses, fungi, or protozoa.

An infection can start in any part of the body, such as on a patch of skin or a wound. If the pathogen only multiplies in this part of the body, we call it a local infection, but if the germs spread around the body, we call it a systemic infection.

When there is an infection, germs can cause disease as they multiply. Some of these pathogens also secrete toxins—substances that damage our body.

When our body defends itself from infection, this can lead to fever, inflammation, pain, coughing, vomiting, or diarrhoea, along with other disease symptoms. If our defenses (👁 p. 50) are strong, we can fight and destroy the germs and cure the infection, although sometimes we need outside help: we have to take medication to help us get rid of the germs.

EXAMPLES OF INFECTIOUS DISEASES

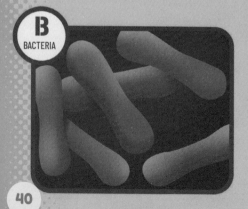

B
BACTERIA

Diphtheria This is a serious disease, caused by a toxin from the bacteria *Corynebacterium diphtheriae*. It usually affects the throat and nose. It is transmitted through direct contact with infected people. Nowadays, hardly anyone becomes infected with diphtheria because we are given a vaccine when we are small.

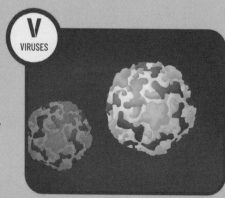

V
VIRUSES

Common cold Bet you've caught one of these before. It is caused by rhinoviruses, the most common pathogens in humans. There is no vaccine or cure, our defenses are capable of beating it. To avoid catching a cold, the best thing to do is wash your hands, use disposable tissues, disinfect your things, and don't get too close to anybody who has one.

Louis Pasteur

Pasteur (1822–1895) was not a doctor but he was a great scientist. His ideas and discoveries have been very important for medical progress and he is considered the pioneer of modern microbiology. One of his most important discoveries was showing that microbes were the cause of many diseases.

In his era, it seemed ridiculous to think that something so insignificantly small like a microorganism could kill much bigger and stronger beings like animals or people.

He spent several years investigating the cause of a disease that was killing silkworms. Thanks to the microscope, he discovered that the silkworms were dying due to a combination of a fungus and various bacteria that infected their larvae and the white mulberry tree leaves they ate. When the infected eggs and leaves were removed, the worms did not catch the disease.

Thanks to these experiments, Pasteur was able to show that infectious diseases were caused by microorganisms.

The silk industry was very important in the south of France, which is why it was so vital to save the worms.

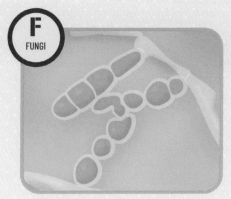

F FUNGI

Tinea This is a skin infection caused by fungi called dermatophytes that take up residence in the skin, hair, and nails. You can catch it from direct contact with the skin of an infected animal or person. We usually treat it with antifungals: a medication that stops the fungi growing.

P PROTOZOA

Sleeping sickness This is a disease caused by a group of parasitical protozoa called *Trypanosoma*. It is transmitted through the bite of an infected tsetse fly. It causes fever, headaches, joint pain, and weakness. It makes people very tired and sleepy and it can be fatal if not treated in time.

WASHING YOUR HANDS

We touch everything with our hands. Hands are a warm and damp surface, with traces of sweat and flakes of skin that act like a magnet for all kinds of microorganisms, both innocuous and pathogenic.

This is why washing your hands with soap and water is necessary to stop bacteria, viruses, and fungi from infecting us.

IGNAZ SEMMELWEIS
(1818-1865)

He was a doctor who discovered that washing our hands very thoroughly saves lives.

He is known as the "savior of mothers." Although his fellow doctors at the time took little notice of him, he showed that disinfecting hands before treating women who were about to give birth stopped them dying from infections.

WHEN SHOULD WE WASH OUR HANDS?

- Before eating and cooking.
- After going to the bathroom.
- After cleaning the house.
- After touching animals, including family pets.
- After visiting or looking after sick friends or family members.
- After blowing your nose, coughing, or sneezing.
- After being outside (playing, gardening, walking the dog, etc.).

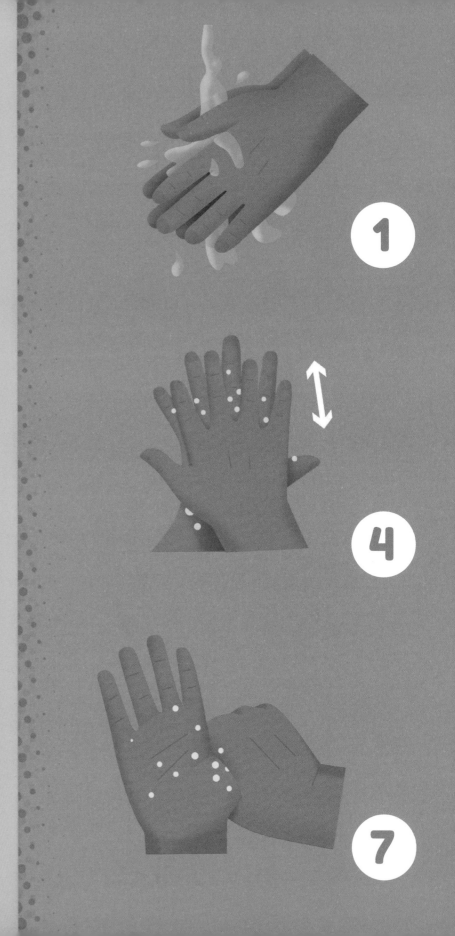

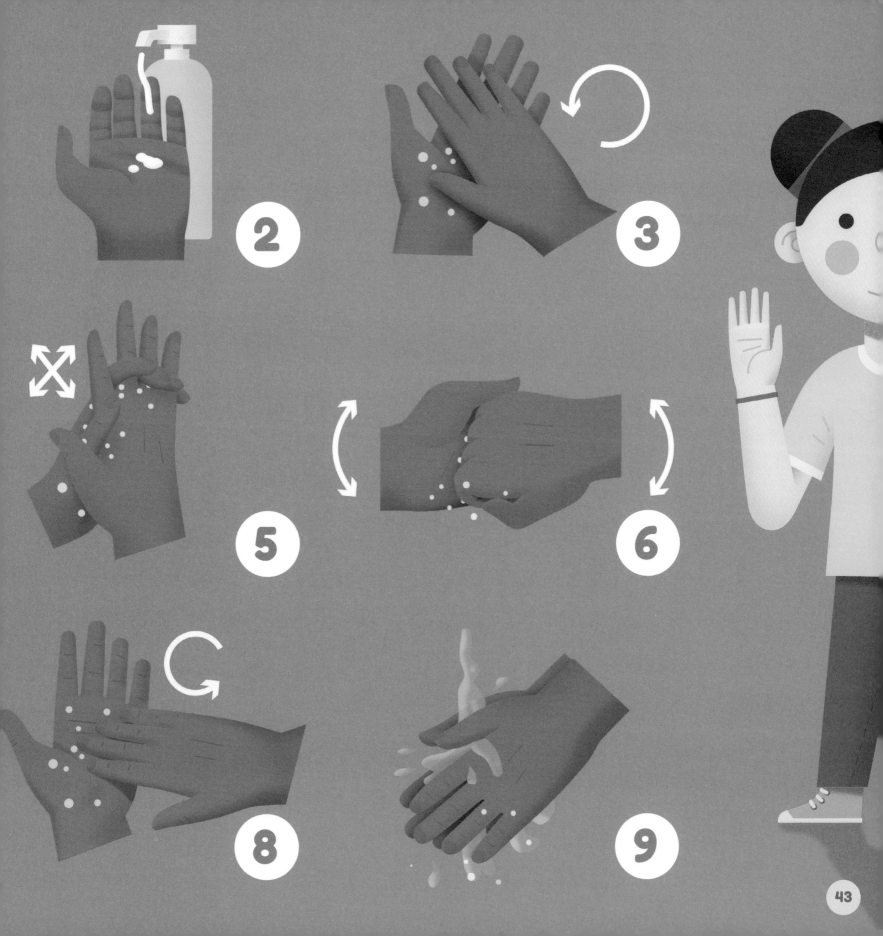

ANTIBIOTICS

An antibiotic is a chemical substance that kills or prevents the growth of some microorganisms.

Antibiotics are usually used as medications to treat infections caused by BACTERIA.

If our defenses (👁 p. 50) cannot contain an infection caused by bacteria, or if they are taking a long time to fight it, we can use antibiotics to help make us healthy again.

Antibiotics are very toxic for bacteria and not very toxic for our cells. This makes them able to kill bacteria with very little harm to us. This is why they are used a lot in medicine.

Throughout history, infections caused by pathogenic bacteria have been one of the major causes of death among humans (👁 p. 60).

Many of the known antibiotics, such as penicillin, are produced naturally by other microorganisms in an attempt to defend themselves against pathogenic bacteria that try to invade them.

ANTIBIOTICS CANNOT BE USED TO CURE INFECTIONS CAUSED BY VIRUSES.

PENICILLIN

This was the first antibiotic used in medicine to treat infections caused by bacteria. Its discovery was a huge step forward for humanity as, since then, it has saved millions of lives.

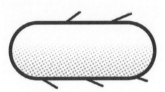

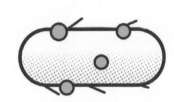

Penicillin acts by weakening the bacterial cell wall so the bacterium can no longer retain everything inside it, and it over-inflates, bursts, and dies.

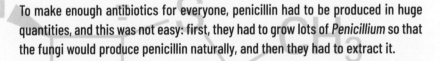

Penicillin was discovered by accident by the Scottish physician and microbiologist Alexander Fleming (1881-1955) in 1928. While studying bacteria in his laboratory, he noticed that one of the cultures containing *Staphylococcus* bacteria had accidentally been contaminated and a fungus called *Penicillium notatum* had grown in it. Instead of throwing the culture away, he decided to look at it under the microscope to see what had happened. He was very surprised to observe that all the *Staphylococci* around the fungus had died. The fungus had produced a substance, an antibiotic that killed bacteria: PENICILLIN.

To make enough antibiotics for everyone, penicillin had to be produced in huge quantities, and this was not easy: first, they had to grow lots of *Penicillium* so that the fungi would produce penicillin naturally, and then they had to extract it.

The scientists Howard W. Florey (1898-1968) and Ernst Chain (1906-1979) helped a lot in the development of penicillin and they confirmed its efficacy for curing bacterial infections. Along with Fleming, they received the Nobel Prize in Physiology or Medicine in 1945.

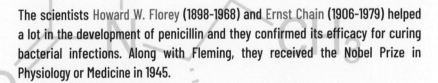

But it wasn't until 1949 that penicillin could be manufactured in large quantities. It was thanks to the scientist Dorothy Hodgkin (1910-1994) who, after years of research, discovered the chemical structure of penicillin. This made it possible to improve the way it was manufactured and to synthesize it in greater quantities in laboratories. Since then, it has been possible to treat people with bacterial infections and millions of lives have been saved. She received the Nobel Prize for Chemistry in 1964.

AS YOU CAN SEE, SCIENCE IS ABOUT GREAT TEAMWORK.

BACTERIAL RESISTANCE

Pathogenic bacteria are astute attackers. Ever since we have been using antibiotics against them, they have been learning to defend themselves.

Many bacteria have found strategies to block the effects of antibiotics: they have developed BACTERIAL RESISTANCE TO ANTIBIOTICS.

But how do they do it?

Different types of antibiotics attack bacteria in different ways. But some bacteria find a way to dodge these chemical attacks.

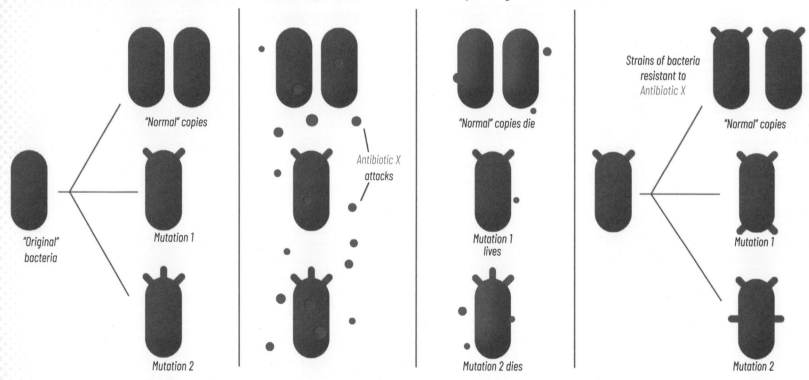

"Normal" copies

Antibiotic X attacks

"Normal" copies die

Strains of bacteria resistant to Antibiotic X

"Normal" copies

"Original" bacteria

Mutation 1

Mutation 1 lives

Mutation 1

Mutation 2

Mutation 2 dies

Mutation 2

MUTATIONS

Bacteria multiply through many cell divisions all day long (👁 p. 18). As they are very simple cells, with each cell division there tend to be small errors in the copying. A new bacterium can be different from the previous one: we say it has mutated.

NATURAL SELECTION

There are lots of divisions, so there are lots of mutations too. Many of these mutations serve no purpose, but some teach the bacteria something new so they can survive in a hostile environment.

If we attack bacteria with antibiotics, the weak ones die and the strong ones become more vigorous. They use mutations to learn how to fight the antibiotic and become resistant.

Some bacteria have learned to make substances called beta-lactamases that are capable of destroying penicillin and other similar antibiotics like amoxicillin, making them no longer effective in treating infections from these bacteria.

As you can imagine, this is a very serious problem for National Health Services as it will get harder and harder to cure infections that before were very easy to treat.

Research is being done into more antibiotics, so that we can fight off pathogenic bacteria once today's antibiotics no longer work.

To ensure the process does not accelerate, and to delay bacterial resistance as much as possible, the best thing to do is to use antibiotics correctly, and only when and how the doctor tells us.

We know of around 200 antibiotics but, little by little, one after the other, they are becoming useless.

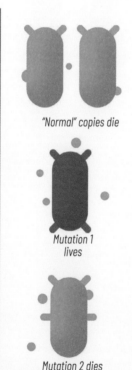

"Normal" copies

Antibiotic Y attacks

Mutation 1

Mutation 2

"Normal" copies die

Mutation 1 lives

Mutation 2 dies

Bacteria resistant to Antibiotic Y *and* Antibiotic X

SUPERBUGS

These bacteria **are resistant to most known antibiotics** and they cause very serious infections. There are more and more superbugs and some are able to pass on the information about resistance to other bacteria that are not resistant, which makes them even more dangerous.

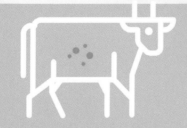

The incorrect use of antibiotics in farm animals also increases bacterial resistance.

Remember that antibiotics are not used to treat viral infections.

TRANSMISSION

Germs can be transmitted from an infected animal or person to another that is not infected. They can do this in many different ways: by direct contact, through the air, through insect bites, through food or drink, and so on.

Malaria

Malaria is a disease caused by parasitic protozoa of the *Plasmodium genus* that is passed on to humans through bites from infected female *Anopheles* mosquitoes.

Measles

It is very infectious. It is passed on through the air when infected people cough or sneeze and expel droplets of saliva containing the measles virus into the air.

Plague

This is a disease caused by the *Yersinia pestis* bacteria that is usually found in small mammals, such as rats, and in the fleas that live and feed off them (parasites). It can become very serious, and has caused major epidemics throughout history (👁 p. 60). It still exists in some countries.

It is transmitted by bites from infected fleas, direct contact with infected fabrics, or by inhaling infected respiratory droplets.

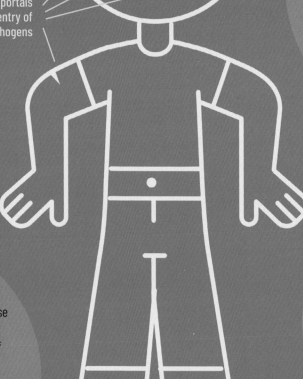

Main portals of entry of pathogens

Salmonellosis

A salmonella infection is a bacterial disease affecting the intestinal tract. Salmonella bacteria generally live in the intestines of humans and animals, although they are also common in the skin of many reptiles. They are released through feces.

Humans are normally infected through contaminated water or food.

Cholera

This is mainly passed on through water contaminated by the *Vibrio cholerae* bacteria. It is typical in areas of bad sanitation where water is contaminated with infected feces.

ROBERT KOCH

(1843-1910)

He was a German physician and microbiologist who became famous thanks to his discovery in 1882 of the bacteria that causes tuberculosis, *Mycobacterium tuberculosis*, also called Koch's bacillus (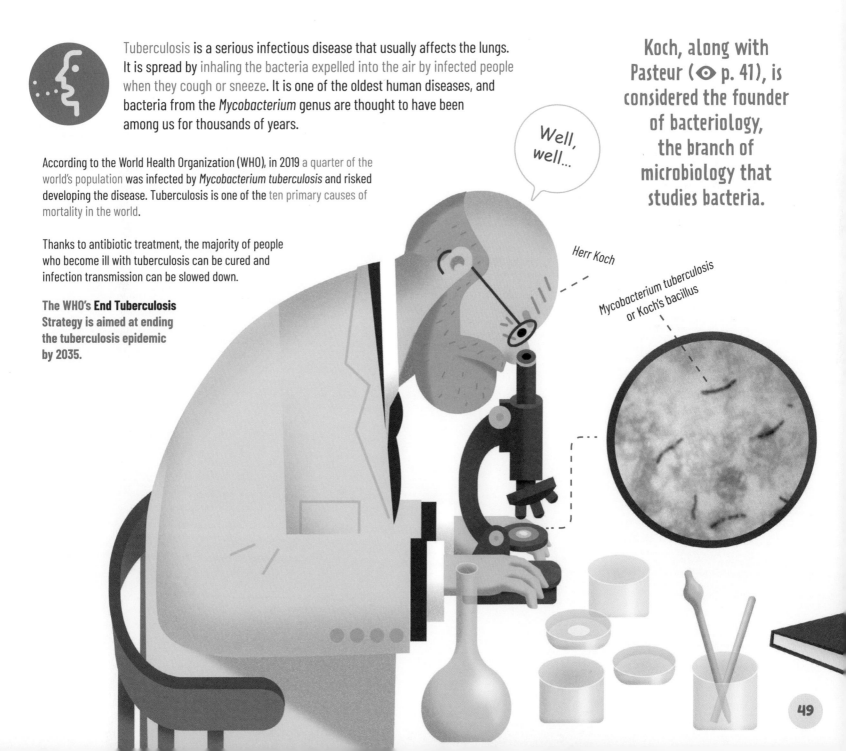 p. 16). He received the Nobel Prize for Physiology or Medicine in 1905 for this discovery.

Tuberculosis is a serious infectious disease that usually affects the lungs. It is spread by inhaling the bacteria expelled into the air by infected people when they cough or sneeze. It is one of the oldest human diseases, and bacteria from the *Mycobacterium* genus are thought to have been among us for thousands of years.

According to the World Health Organization (WHO), in 2019 a quarter of the world's population was infected by *Mycobacterium tuberculosis* and risked developing the disease. Tuberculosis is one of the ten primary causes of mortality in the world.

Thanks to antibiotic treatment, the majority of people who become ill with tuberculosis can be cured and infection transmission can be slowed down.

The WHO's **End Tuberculosis Strategy** is aimed at ending the tuberculosis epidemic by 2035.

Koch, along with Pasteur (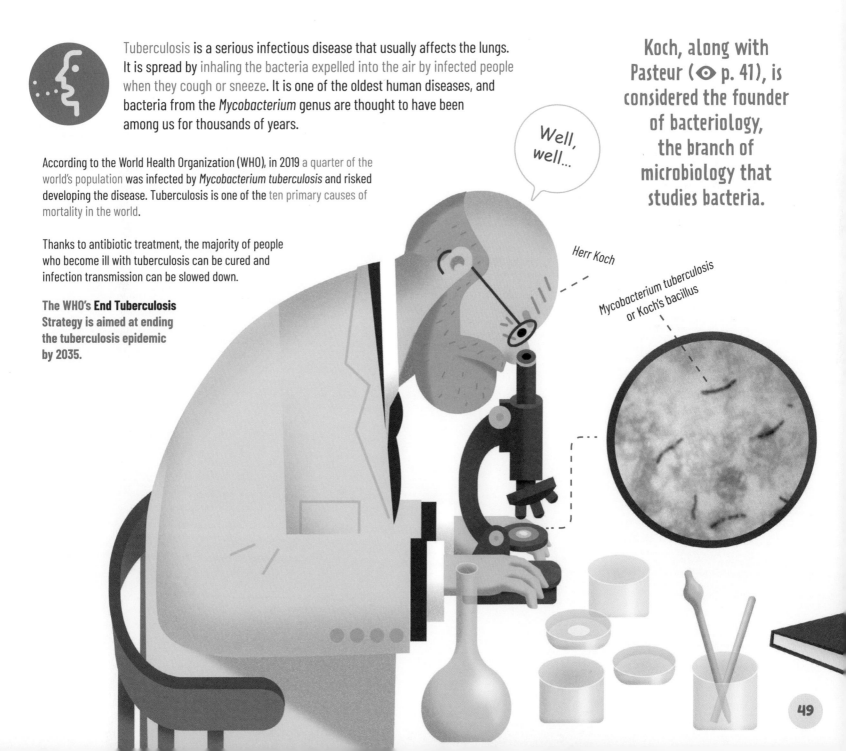 p. 41), is considered the founder of bacteriology, the branch of microbiology that studies bacteria.

Well, well...

Herr Koch

Mycobacterium tuberculosis or Koch's bacillus

OUR DEFENSES

We are barely aware of this, but every day we are waging a war against an invading army. Every second of our lives, our body is being attacked by enemy microorganisms: bacteria, viruses, fungi, protozoa. To defend us, our body can rely on a very sophisticated defense system, the IMMUNE SYSTEM, which protects us from these invaders.

An army of leukocytes

The immune system has a huge army formed of billions of LEUKOCYTES, white blood cells, in which every type of cell has specific tasks.

YOUR HEALTH

VIRUS

If we have a wound, bacteria might try to penetrate this initial barrier. Given that bacteria duplicate every 20 minutes (👁 p. 18), after a few hours they can take control of the area and this can then become an invasion.

This is why the immune system has to intervene to stop the invasion.

Wound

Soldiers

Macrophages, granulocytes, natural killer cells. Their job is to patrol, perform phagocytosis (devour), and kill enemies.

Our first defense is our skin because it is a natural barrier like a wall and, what's more, it secretes substances that are harmful to any invaders attempting to get through it.

1st line of battle

Neutrophil

The first to arrive at the infected area are MACROPHAGES, which are capable of swallowing around 100 bacteria each.

What's more, they send signals from the cells damaged by the invasion to the blood vessels to get them to release water, and the area becomes inflamed. This makes it easier for reinforcements to arrive on the battlefield in the blood. Sometimes, macrophages can stamp out the attack on their own. But if things get more complicated, they ask for help from the neutrophils, very aggressive warriors capable of killing the enemy and causing a lot of damage in the area.

Red blood cell

Reconnaissance patrols

Dendritic cells

Their job is to detect the enemy and inform headquarters, so that reinforcements are sent to the battlefront. They give pieces of the dead enemy to the intelligence services so they can study it.

2nd line of battle

If complications develop with the infection, and the intruders have not been stopped, a very sophisticated defense system comes into play, the specific immune response, whose job is to identify, confront, and remember the enemy for future invasions.

The dendritic cells arrive on the battlefield to pick up pieces of the enemy and take them to the nearest headquarters (lymphatic ganglion) where they meet the T lymphocytes, the immune system's intelligence services.

Intelligence services headquarters (lymphatic ganglions)

Once the enemy has been analyzed, some T lymphocytes go to the battlefield to help and to coordinate the conflict, others are converted into memory cells to remember the enemy for future invasions, and others activate the B lymphocytes that manufacture a very powerful weapon, the antibodies.

Antibodies are like guided missiles designed specifically for each enemy. Antibodies can deactivate the intruder by binding to it, making it die, or "tagging" it so that other immune system cells can recognize and eliminate it more efficiently.

Intelligence

T lymphocytes pass on detailed information about the enemy, give orders to all the other cells to coordinate attacks and organize the defenses, and order the production of armaments.

Arms factories

B lymphocytes manufacture antibodies.

This second line of defense arrives on the battlefront to reinforce the defenses with millions of antibodies that kill or weaken the intruders. The infection subsides as more and more bacteria die until finally none are left alive.

MEMORY CELLS
IMMUNIZATION

As we have seen, after a pathogen (a virus for example) triggers a dangerous infection for the first time (primary), our organism generates T lymphocytes and B lymphocytes to defend us. These are cells that specialize in combating this particular invader.

The pathogen enters our body and the battle begins.

If the infection persists, the immune system creates lymphocytes.

The lymphocytes analyze the enemy and create antibodies as required.

The immune system fires its antibodies at the invader until it is defeated.

 Our body needs several days to generate lymphocytes, which is why it can take days or weeks to recover from a primary infection and be cured.

And after that?

While the immune system is fighting an infection, it does something pretty ingenious, it generates MEMORY cells: T lymphocytes and B lymphocytes that remember the invader, in this case, a virus. Once the infection is vanquished these cells do not disappear. They carry on patrolling around our body in case a "known" enemy appears again.

They are a very efficient intelligence service that mobilizes instantly: as soon as a new infection caused by the same virus occurs, the memory cells recognize it and immediately generate a quick and strong immune response. In very little time, antibodies against the virus are generated and the immune system cells are given orders to attack. The infection is stamped out and the virus is eliminated without us even realizing.

When we have memory cells against a pathogen, we are said to be

IMMUNIZED

against this pathogen: it can no longer make us sick.

When we beat infections, we usually become immune. Sometimes that is for life, as is the case with the measles virus, but occasionally the situation is different and we are only immune for a while (a few months or years); for example, the flu virus can change slightly from year to year, so the memory cells will not recognize it.

As we go through life and beat different infectious diseases, our immune system gets stronger and stronger, "collecting" memory cells of the diseases we have had.

This is why when we are small we are often unwell, because we don't yet have enough memory cells.

But is there any way that our body can produce memory cells against a pathogen we have never come into contact with? Fighting viruses and bacteria can be a risky business, especially if our body is up against particularly "virulent" microbes.

Can we be immunized without having to go into battle against the dangerous pathogens? Yes we can, with

VACCINES

VACCINES

A vaccine is a clever way to trick our body into producing memory cells and immunizing us against a particular infectious disease WITHOUT US GETTING SICK.

As we have seen, our immune system defends itself against infections by studying pieces of dead microbes and producing specific antibodies. This information is stored in our immune system's memory cells, creating an "archive" that makes it possible to quickly recognize the invader and immediately attack it.

This is what we call a VACCINE: a medication made from dead or weakened microorganisms (normally bacteria and viruses) that our immune system can capture, study, and remember without danger of infecting us, and this makes us immune to future infections.

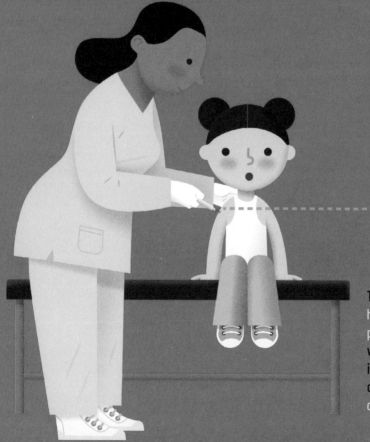

To achieve this, we introduce half-dead pathogens or pieces of pathogens into our body, in such a way that they cannot harm us. Our immune system is able to fight them off very easily and generate memory cells that produce antibodies.

So if we come across this pathogen at some point and it tries to infect us, our body is prepared to fight off the infection. We have become immune without ever having fallen ill because of this pathogen.

The first vaccine in history

In the late 18th century, an English physician and scientist, **Edward Jenner (1749–1823)**, realized that people who milked cows never caught smallpox, one of the most fatal diseases for humankind ( p. 59).

"I shall never have smallpox for I have had cowpox," Jenner overheard one of the local milkmaids say.

The milkmaids were immune because they had already been sick with the cowpox virus, which is much less aggressive than the human smallpox virus. Their bodies remembered how to defend themselves against the cowpox virus, so they knew what to do when attacked by the human smallpox virus.

On May 14th 1796, Jenner injected a liquid containing cowpox virus into an eight-year-old boy called James Phipps. James could not then become infected with smallpox. He was immunized.

The word "vaccine" comes from "vacca," "cow" in Latin.

Nowadays, there are vaccines against quite a lot of infectious diseases, such as measles, mumps, chickenpox, hepatitis A and B, flu, rabies, diphtheria, tetanus, whooping cough, yellow fever, cholera, and polio among others.

Throughout history, infectious diseases, especially those caused by viruses and bacteria, have killed millions of people. Thanks to the vaccination of the population, many, many lives have been saved.

But not all infectious diseases, such as AIDS for example, have a vaccine yet. This is why scientists are still researching to find vaccines for diseases that do not yet have one.

Imagine you have heard such a juicy rumor that you can't help telling someone else. You don't much like gossip, but you decide to tell only your best friend and no one else.

The next day, your friend does the same and they tell someone else.

If everyone who hears the rumor decided to do the same, it would spread, though NOT that much: after a month, only 30 people would have heard it.

DAY 1	DAY 2	DAY 3	DAY 4	DAY 5	DAY 6	DAY 7	DAY 30
1	2	3	4	5	6	7	

30 PEOPLE

1   3   7   15   31   63   127

But what if instead of telling one friend, you tell two? That wouldn't add up to very many people either, would it? The first day, 1 person would know, the second, 3 people, the third, 7...

And if we carry on like that, after a month, more than 1 billion people would have heard it; 1,073,741,823, to be precise.

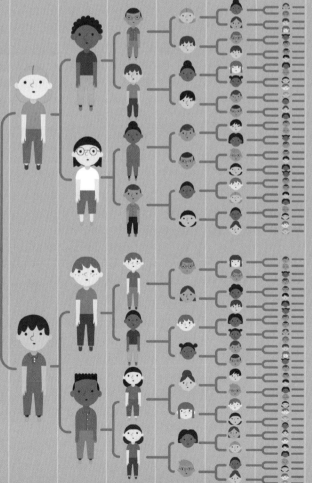

1,073,741,823 PEOPLE

With infectious diseases (the ones caused by pathogens such as bacteria or viruses), something similar to these rumors happens. Depending on the disease, one person can infect one or more people.

Less contagious

$R_0=1$

If the disease has an $R_0=1$, it means that every person infects only one other person, so the disease does not spread very much. After a month, only 30 people would be infected. The spread is said to be linear (based on the shape on the graph).

An **EPIDEMIC** happens when a **disease affects more people than normal in a population over a determined period of time**.

The basic reproduction number (R_0) of the disease is the average number of new infections one person generates while they are infectious.

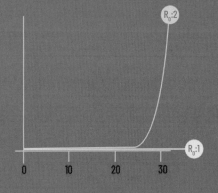

$R_0:2$

$R_0:1$

0   10   20   30

An epidemic usually appears in a given geographical area, like a city, a region, or country. When the epidemic spreads across several continents, or even around the world, it is then called a PANDEMIC.

Whereas, if the disease has an $R_0=2$, it spreads very quickly. After a month, there would be billions of people infected. In this case, it spreads exponentially.

$R_0=2$

The higher the R_0 number of an infectious disease outbreak in a certain population, the more likely it is to become an epidemic and the more difficult it will be to contain.

Imagine an EPIDEMIC with an R_0 number of 4!

More contagious

57

Imagine that Lina has caught a flu virus with an $R_0=2$.
As we've already seen, this could be a bit of a disaster because lots of people could be infected in a short time and it could become an epidemic.

Ideally, a disease should have an $R_0=1$ or less; in other words, each person infects a maximum of one other.

Vaccines help us decrease the R_0 rate of the disease as they immunize people and make sure they cannot be infected.

Let's look at it using our example:

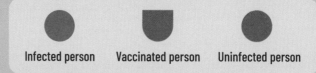

Infected person   Vaccinated person   Uninfected person

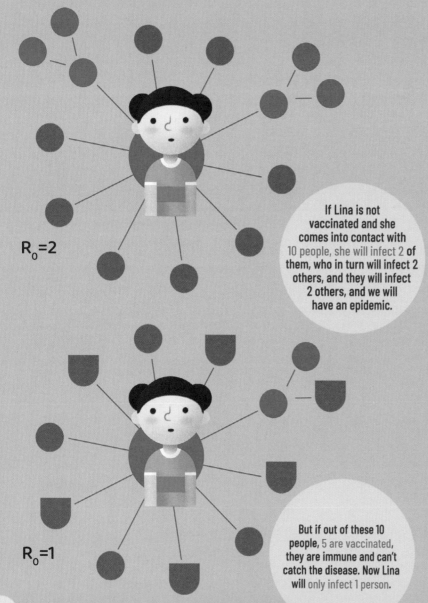

$R_0=2$

If Lina is not vaccinated and she comes into contact with 10 people, she will infect 2 of them, who in turn will infect 2 others, and they will infect 2 others, and we will have an epidemic.

$R_0=1$

But if out of these 10 people, 5 are vaccinated, they are immune and can't catch the disease. Now Lina will only infect 1 person.

So if we vaccinate just half of the population, we reduce the R_0 number of our flu virus from 2 to 1 and the spread of the disease goes from exponential to linear.

HERD IMMUNITY

Our flu now has much more trouble infecting people so it spreads more slowly and it cannot become an epidemic.

Although the other half of the population is not immunized, they are protected because it would be much harder for them to be infected thanks to those who have been vaccinated. We have reached HERD IMMUNITY.

Of course, the greater the quantity of people in the population that are vaccinated, the greater the herd immunity will be.

People who are cured of an infectious disease and become immune, also contribute to herd immunity.

ERADICATED DISEASES

Thanks to vaccines, we have been able to do something even better: eradicate a disease; in other words, make it disappear, which is what happened with smallpox.

SMALLPOX

Smallpox is a very serious contagious disease that is caused by the *Variola virus*. It first emerged in human populations around 12,000 years ago. It kills 3 out of 10 people who catch it and it is very contagious, with an R_0 number of 5. 😨😨😨😨😨

It is one of the most deadly diseases that humans have ever known; it has infected and killed hundreds of millions of people throughout history.

Thanks to vaccination campaigns from the mid-20th century onwards, and also to information and prevention work, the disease has been successfully isolated and vanquished. The last recorded case of naturally acquired smallpox was in 1977. In 1980, the WHO declared it officially eradicated.

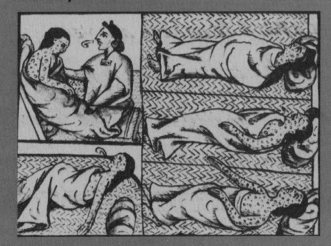

Smallpox epidemics that the Spanish conquistadors carried with them were one of the biggest causes of the demographic catastrophe in the Americas from 1492 onwards.

Great Epidemics and Pandemics in History

An epidemic occurs when a contagious disease spreads rapidly in a given population, simultaneously affecting a large number of people over a given period of time. If an epidemic affects widespread geographical areas (for example, several continents), it then becomes a pandemic.

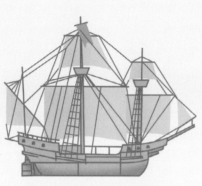

One of the ways this plague was transmitted was through the bite of infected fleas. The fleas often traveled on the rats aboard merchant ships, so ports were major centers of infection.

Antonine Plague
(165–180CE)

5 M

The Antonine Plague or the Plague of Galen (after the name of the doctor who described it) was a smallpox or measles pandemic that infected the entire Roman Empire. It is estimated to have caused 5 million deaths, 10% of the population.

Justinian Plague
(541–750CE)

This was a plague epidemic that ravaged the Byzantium Empire between 541 and 543. There were various waves until approximately the year 750, and it spread across Africa, Asia, and Europe. It is estimated that between 25 and 50 million people died.

25–50 M

The doctors who treated the plague victims were dressed like this. A beak-shaped mask contained aromatic herbs to filter the air they were breathing, as it was believed the disease "floated" in the air.

Common flea, which transmitted the *Yersinia pestis* bacteria that caused the plague.

Black Death
(14th century)

This plague epidemic was one of the most devastating in the history of humanity. It affected Asia and Europe in the 14th century and reached a peak between 1347 and 1353. It is thought to have originated in Asia and from there spread across the trade routes to Europe where it hit hard, killing a third of the continent's population.

25–50 M

Demographic catastrophe in the Americas (1492)

The European conquistadors took many diseases to the Americas against which the natives had no immune defenses. Smallpox, measles, and syphilis were much more lethal than weapons. It is estimated that 95% of the total population of the Americas died from diseases following the arrival of Columbus.

12–15 M

Cholera (1817–1896)   *Vibrio cholerae*

The first pandemic began in Calcutta in 1817, spreading to the whole of India, and, in the following years, to the whole world. The various waves of cholera caused by the presence of the *Vibrio cholerae* bacillus in water decimated the global population.

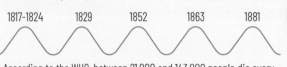

1817-1824   1829   1852   1863   1881

10 M

According to the WHO, between 21,000 and 143,000 people die every year from cholera.

Spanish Flu

(1918–1920)

`Influenza A (H1N1) virus`

The First World War was not yet over when this flu spread around the world. Despite the name, it didn't start in Spain but in the USA. It is considered the most deadly pandemic in modern history, killing around 40 million people in 1918-1919, much more than the number of people who died in the war. Unlike seasonal flu, the majority of its victims were young. The strangest (and most mysterious) thing is that in 1920 the virus disappeared almost without a trace as quickly as it had appeared two years previously.

40 M

Mutations of the flu virus cause serious pandemics. Seasonal flu also causes thousands of deaths every year, especially in more vulnerable populations, the elderly, and small children.

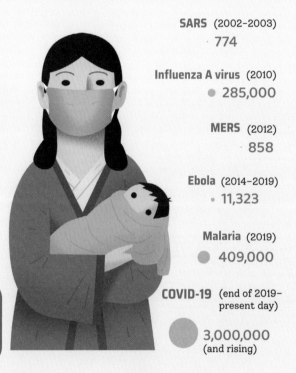

SARS (2002-2003)
774

Influenza A virus (2010)
285,000

MERS (2012)
858

Ebola (2014-2019)
11,323

Malaria (2019)
409,000

COVID-19 (end of 2019–present day)
3,000,000 (and rising)

Measles (👁 p. 48)
`Paramyxovirus`

This used to be one of humanity's most deadly diseases, causing more than 200 million deaths. The WHO estimates that between 2000 and 2017, 21 million deaths were prevented thanks to the vaccine.

200 M

Smallpox (👁 p. 59)
`Variola virus`

This is the most deadly disease in history. In 18th-century Europe, it is estimated that around 400,000 people died every year from smallpox, and a third of the survivors went blind. It killed up to 300 million people in its last 100 years of existence alone. The disease was successfully eradicated thanks to the vaccine.

500 M

Asian Flu
(1957–1958)
`Influenza A (H3N2) virus`
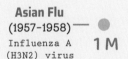 1 M

Hong Kong Flu
(1969)
`Influenza A (H2N2) virus`
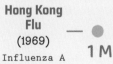 1 M

Russian Flu
(1889–1890)
`Influenza A (H3N8) virus`
1 M

AIDS
`Human immunodeficiency virus (HIV)`

This virus attacks the immune system of infected people, leaving them with no defenses against diseases.

32 M

COVID-19

Coronaviruses (CoV) are a family of viruses that can cause different illnesses, from a common cold to more serious diseases such as COVID-19, which is caused by a new coronavirus called SARS-CoV-2 that had not been detected before in humans.

It is very contagious and spreads mostly through the air by people inhaling micro-droplets containing the virus, which are exhaled by infected people when they breathe, talk, or cough (that's why it's so important to wear masks).

MASK   DISTANCING   HYGIENE

When the virus enters the body, it uses its spike proteins (S proteins) to attach to the ACE2 receptors in some cells, such as lung cells.

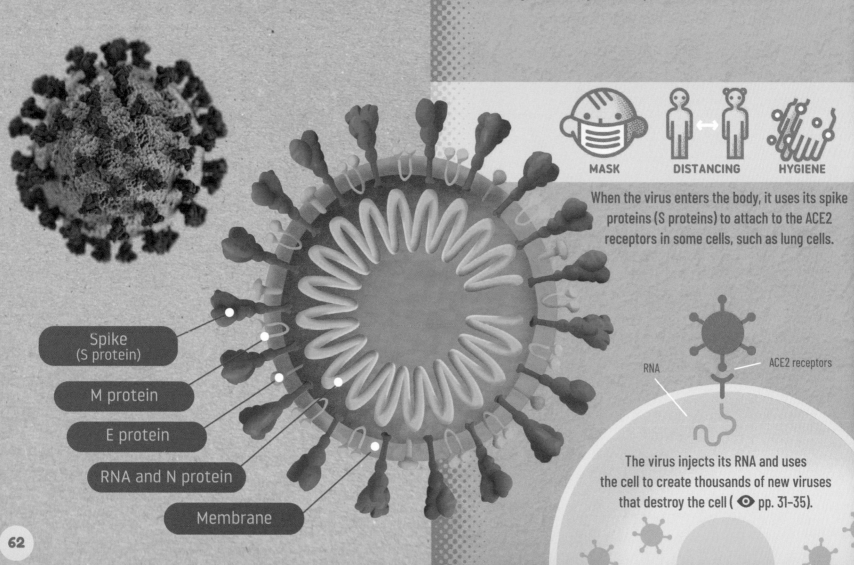

Spike (S protein)

M protein

E protein

RNA and N protein

Membrane

RNA

ACE2 receptors

The virus injects its RNA and uses the cell to create thousands of new viruses that destroy the cell (👁 pp. 31–35).